NATIONAL GEOGRAPHIC

T0072238

What's on the Road?

Norman Yu

What's on the road?

Table of Contents

Cars 4
Motorcycles 5
Buses 6
Trucks 7
People 8

There are cars on the road.

There are **motorcycles** on the road.

There are **buses** on the road.

There are **trucks** on the road.

There are **people** on the road.